Touching the Hearts of Pastors' Wives

A Conversation

By Dr. Judy Ellison

ISBN 979-8-88680-742-4

Touching the Hearts of Pastors' Wives

Table of Contents

INTRODUCTION

My purpose for sharing my book Touching the Hearts of Pastors' Wives is to enlighten you that countless women share similar concerns and trials as you do. In addition, we are still fighting to overcome them. Over the years, I talked with many pastors' wives who shared incredible and hurtful stories with me. When you read this book, I pray that you will be motivated to keep pressing beyond your present circumstances while believing God and other pastors' wives to reach new heights in God.

DEDICATION

To all the women serving in ministry, thank you for many prayers. To my children for allowing me to have the spare time to author this book. To my husband, who helps me become that woman God can use. To Annie Fuller, who worked hard in typing and proofreading the manuscript repeatedly. Thanks for believing in me.

CHAPTER 1
Ministering To Your Mate

A pastor's wife should be worthy of her calling, and her call is to walk beside, not behind or in front of, the man of God. She is to be that helpmeet which God intended. Be certain that it is an extremely high <u>call,</u> and we as pastors' wives should not take it lightly. Why? Because the call is from God. With strong dedication and consecration to the Lord, we can be all God wants us to be. Only then will we become an asset to our husbands. Along with your husband's call from God, you have one, too.

Our lives are often juggling everything from women's groups to marketing. Yet, our priorities are our husbands and children. Let us not forget that we are helpers. That means doing whatever it takes to relax him so he can hear from God. God will reward you greatly. Let us make our home a heaven for our man so that God will be pleased.

Many pastors' wives say they do not know what God called them to do. I know we can be useful in many areas, especially counseling women and girls. There will always be times when they need to have intimate talks and advice that only you could give freely. A woman knows women and can better help the ladies in her church. Also, know that we will counsel women we do not feel comfortable around. However, we must be able to give them loving and compassionate guidance. A good wife is a great blessing to her husband and children. That is our first responsibility, then ministry. Let us keep our priorities in the right order.

Pastors' wives do not make it easy for Satan to

find a way of stealing your husband. Hold tightly to him yet give him space. He is your responsibility! No other woman can care for him like you do. Let him find security in your love and trust. Make sacrifices if necessary to keep the romance in your marriage.

You should be a good <u>lover</u> to your husband and keep a good relationship going. This will save your husband from temptations exposed in his leadership position. Our husband might be a great man of faith and power, but he is still <u>human</u>. He has physical, emotional, spiritual, and psychological needs like any other human being. To keep your marriage happy and avoid unnecessary pain, we must do our best to keep the romance in the marriage. In other words, give him plenty of sex!

Listed below are things we must do daily to maintain personal and private devotions with the

Lord. First, a pastor's wife must pray for her husband, children, and church. Secondly, she must avoid gossip and slander and be sure to not counsel men alone. Thirdly, never insult your husband publicly. Differences should be settled at home. Away from home, respect and honor your husband in every way possible. Lastly, avoid sensuous and sensitive dressing in public. This will communicate a wrong message and easily hurt you and your husband's ministry. People will always look for you to be role models.

CHAPTER 2
Adjusting to the Role of a Pastor's Wife

Years ago, my husband and I were called by God to pastor the Oasis of Hope Church. Along with my husband, I was excited about this new assignment from the Lord. There is just a profound sense of expectation and anticipation that comes to us when we know that God is calling us to an area we have never been before. This area is what I call unknown territory. However, along with the excitement to obey God comes the fears of the unknown and the time of adjustment.

You and I know that we must face our fears so they do not paralyze us and cause us to be disobedient to the will of God. These fears range from being accepted by your peers, being accepted by the congregation, and adjusting to your husband's expectations as a pastor's wife. You can overcome your fears with the knowledge of what God has said about you and what he wants to do through you.

As in every new thing in line, there is always the necessity for adjustments, so it is in the role of a pastor's wife. Take note of things we have to adjust to in life: a marriage, a new baby, a career, a new house, and the list could go on and on. Adjustment time should never be looked at as wasted time because it is necessary for all levels of growth. As a pastor's wife, we must adjust ourselves in two principal areas: firstly, to our husbands' expectations, and secondly, to the role of a pastor's wife concerning the congregation.

The Word adjust means "to change to match or

fit or conform to new conditions." The Lord wants us to be willing to adjust to whatever assignment he may send our way. If you are a pastor's wife, I encourage you to submit your will to the Lord so he can strengthen you for your adjustment. Please, ladies, know that if you are married to a pastor, then it is no coincidence and God's will for you is to make necessary adjustments. It can be a transitional time of growth for you or a nightmare, depending on your willingness to conform to God's known will for you at the time. The first main adjustment area is your husband as a pastor and leader. Please realize that he has to undergo adjustment as well as you do and that God has called both of you to adjust at the same time to your positions. I have personally found out that we should ask our husbands, "What are your expectations of me?" Also, ask him, "What are my freedoms and limitations?" After all, we want to be an asset and not a liability. Secondly, we must adjust (change and match) our role as an example before the congregation.

Many of you have become frustrated and disappointed as a pastor's wife. With the help of the Lord and our husbands, we can develop a healthy, working relationship with the congregation. Still, I must tell you that a lot of the heartache has come out of not knowing how to adjust. When it comes to adjusting to the role of a pastor's wife, we must know what God has said about us and what he wants to do through us is greater than the fears and oppositions we will face. Notice, I did say you will face fears and oppositions; however, do not be afraid and remember what the Lord said many times in the scriptures, "Fear not." Isaiah 41:10 declares, "Fear thou not; for I am with thee: be not dismayed; for I am thy God: I will strengthen; yea, I will help thee." Praise God! What a comforting scripture to us as pastors' wives.

Let us talk more about adjusting. The Word adjust means "to fit in, adapt to or blend in or with." Adjusting is something that will occur at each stage. Therefore, if I adjust well at stage one, the pattern will be set to adjust well at stage two. It is like this: if I, as a pastor's wife, can work well with my husband and the congregation (when there are fifty People in our church), I will not have such a tough time adjusting well with one hundred people. With this being the case, we as pastors' wives must maintain an intimate walk with God and our husbands. Let us deal with the God issue first.

The bible says concerning our need for God, "Without Me (Jesus), you can do nothing." We can only produce for God to the degree we are intimate with our husbands; ladies, we must work hard to keep the line of communication open. We can know what is in his heart by communicating with our husbands because he will not mind sharing his heart. Many husbands refuse to share their hearts because they either do not trust their wives, feel they cannot handle what needs to be shared, or feel they will misinterpret what they say. My point is that we must do all we can to help keep the lines of communication open.

If we seek God continually, he will show us how to keep communication flowing. When your husband does open up to you, you must respond in a godly manner, assisting him with what he believes God has told him. That is, you share in his vision. God has a way of exalting us as women when we do what we do as unto the Lord, obediently following the authority of our head. Take the story of Esther, for example. Before Esther, Queen Vashti did not respond to her husband's authority and requests when he desired her the most. She was doing "her own thing," like some of us have been doing. We must remember that we were called helpmates for our husbands. Therefore, we must be ready to help in any situation we can. This was not the case with Vashti, and, therefore, her actions caused her to lose out in the Kingdom.

We have a God-given position as pastors' wives, but we must learn to adjust and flow with our "leader-husbands" to fulfill our destinies. Our focus must not be on what we feel God had called us to do (especially if we know we had a call from God before we got married), but it must be on how we should

flow with our mates. God has a way of bringing forth what he has invested in us if we work to promote our husbands' vision (our vision together under his leadership). Let us remember that what you cause to happen for others, God will cause to happen to you. Now back to the story of Esther. Esther was completely different from Vashti. She prepared herself and stayed ready for the king at his request. You can see that this attitude caused great promotion to come in her life. Notice what the king said to her at one of their banquets:

And the king said unto Esther at the banquet of wine, what is thy petition? And it shall have granted thee: and what is thy request? Even to the half of the Kingdom, it shall be performed. Esther 5:6

Girly, girl, you'd better know she had touched his heart. That kind of honor is available for us if we learn to adjust and flow with our husbands. Reality tells us that there were adjusting times for Esther. I am sure she had her difficult days. Remember Esther was an orphan raised by her uncle (a Jew) in a heathen land, yet God raised her to be a Queen to a heathen king. Now you know that required adjustments. If Esther could adjust to a heathen, we can adjust to a Holy Ghost-filled man. The king's heart (your man) is in the hand of the Lord, and He will turn it.

Women of God get in trouble when we try to turn it. Know that when you try to forcefully change his mind, he does not budge. He does not budge because God created our men with an ego. A God-given ego. If it appears that you are trying to lead, then there will be a conflict of interest. He will rise up to defend his position, and we do not want to get into a battle with him, but we want him to listen to our advice. God has given us many ways to get his attention. One way is the power of sex! Use it for your advantage, not to manipulate. Another way is to become a particularly good listener. They often do not want our opinions but instead have us be good listeners.

CHAPTER 3
How to Adjust to your Role

And wisdom and knowledge shall be the stability of thy times, and strength of salvation. Isaiah 33:6

Since the role of a pastor's wife is so important in a local church, it is extremely important to know "how to adjust" to the role. I have talked to many pastors' wives who were frustrated and wanted out of being a pastor's wife simply because of not knowing how to fit in and make things work. Let me encourage you with the thought that all things are possible with God. You can learn to fit in. Several factors will contribute to our adjustment into the role of a pastor's wife. First of all, we can adjust by asking

God for help. Proverbs 3:5-6 declares:

Trust in the Lord with all thine heart and lean not unto thine own understanding. In all thy ways acknowledge him, and he shall direct thy paths.

We often carry heavy loads and frustrations because of not "casting all our cares on God" in prayer. We need the Lord's help in our adjustment. The problem with many pastors' wives is that they do not have a strong relationship with God themselves. They just depend on the husband's walk with God to be sufficient. Ladies, your husband's walk with God is not enough. You have to be intimate with God for yourself to adjust to your role. Your husband's role is not like your role. Therefore, you will need God's help, strength, and wisdom to successfully accomplish what God and your husband expect of you. By spending quality time with God in prayer and studying his Word, the Holy Spirit will enable you to adjust and effectively function in your role.

The second contributing factor to your adjustment is your husband. It is important to have a good marriage before entering pastoral responsibilities. If a woman does not work hard to flow with her husband, she will have an extremely tough time adjusting as a pastor's wife. Your husband will know where God is taking the ministry and the various things that need to be done. Therefore, we as wives need to be available and willing to help out.

Since we are at this point, you need to be confident that no one can assist your husband like you can. You may encounter smarter women than you and can do things better in some areas (who may try to intimidate you), but still, you are the wife of your husband, the Pastor. Be assured that you carry more influence than any other woman in the church as your husband's wife. So then, use your influence to glorify God and make your husband look good. The final contributing factor that I want to share with you is having a mentor. In every occupation, a mentor is needed. A mentor can help by coaching you into adjustment. Your mentor can save you from many needless mistakes and help you get adjusted a lot quicker than you could have adjusted by yourself. A mentor will also promote real growth and change and provide you with a model to follow.

CHAPTER 4
Why Should a Pastor's Wife Be Active in Ministry?

She should be active because she can add flavor and color to the ministry. She can do a variety of things to assist the ministry. The uniqueness of her part is so especially important. Take, for example, the role of parents. Without the mom, the dad's role is harder. The Lord designed the dad and mom to work as a team in the family. So, when one mate is absent or not functioning, it strains the family. So, it is when a pastor's wife is not functioning or is absent from ministry.

Many women want to be active. They do not want to stagnate and feel insignificant. Still, you, as husbands, senior pastors, in particular, have to tell them what to do or what part to play. Most times, if you pay close attention to her, you will find out what she could do with the purpose and plan that God has given to you as the head of the church. The head is so important, but it takes the neck to turn the head. They work together. We need each other as joints that supply one another. Ephesians 4:26 says:

From whom the whole body fitly joined together and compacted by that which every joint supplieth, according to the effectual working in the measure of every part, maketh increase of the body unto the edifying of itself in love.

When every part is at work, the job is easier. There must be an agreement on what part will be played by whom. If there is no agreement, then there is no blessing. God commands blessings when he sees unity.

Wives, we need to know what part God called us to, and our husbands can help find our part. Please, husbands, do not make her feel like she is insignificant; instead, make her feel important. Show her she is a joy and not a burden. Remember, you are the one that cultivates. We do not come readily prepared in ministry and cultivated as a wife. We must work on each other. Why? Because your wife knows what you need, and you know what she needs. Please note this - the devil does not want to see husbands and wives working together in ministry. In fact, his aim is to keep husbands and wives from working together in anything. It is a fact that working together creates a bonding. Working together in the ministry can help keep the door to infidelity closed.

Ladies, know this, a man has the drive to succeed. That is a part of them that God created. Whoever is there being a "cheerleader" is the one he will tend to bond to because he sees her there to help him succeed. Therefore, it is good that we are there to bond instead of someone else.

When bonding occurs, people really do not intend to fall, but it is a big chance to fall into sexual sins. Here is an example of what happened when the bond was not there. I heard of a pastor with great intentions to walk with God, and he had a secretary, and they were at church alone by themselves a lot. Without him thinking about it, they slept together in the secretary's office. We as wives cannot sit passively and say "let someone else do it" or get so frustrated with a ministry that we do not want to do anything. God's grace is sufficient for you, and his strength is

---

made perfect in your weakness. II Corinthians 12:9 says:

And he said unto me, My grace is sufficient for thee: for my strength is made perfect in weakness. Most gladly, therefore, will I rather glory in my infirmities, that the power of Christ may rest upon me.

We are the protectors of one another as companions!

CHAPTER 5
The Integrity of a Pastor's Wife

As a pastor's wife, I have had many life experiences. Those experiences have taught me to depend fully on God and His Word. My husband once said that he has to (to a certain measure) change the number of people who come through the church doors. Because a pastor and his wife are one, a wife will undergo growth changes with her husband.

A pastor's wife has to go through her measure of change (along with her husband) to continue effectively ministering to the church. I believe that if a wife works closely with her husband, then the two of them will grow close together in trying times instead of apart. Most of all, we must please God the Father who has called us into our position.

I want you to know that this does not have to happen. The devil's plot destroys the intimacy between a pastor and his wife. There are precious qualities that a wife can walk in that will help her to be a godly pastor's wife instead of one who is a thorn to her husband and the work of God.

The first quality is that of **integrity.** This has to do with being sincere and honest. We must be real with ourselves and not phony. God is not expecting us to be like our husbands, but he is expecting us to walk in uprightness as an example. Let us remember Pastor's wives that we are examples for the ladies in our churches. They will tend to pattern their lives after the way we live ours.

The second quality is that of courage. Courage is bravery in the face of fears, dangers, and opposition. Truly, it will require God's courage for us to be able to stand and keep moving forward. Without courage, we will tend to draw back and allow fear to paralyze us. You may say, where can I get that? Well, God's Word is full of it. Go to God's Word and look at examples in the scripture and follow their actions until God's courage begins to work in you.

The third quality is that of vision. You must see yourself as a mighty pastor's wife. Eleanor Roosevelt was a mighty woman who walked with her husband, President Franklin D. Roosevelt. If she could do that in the natural realm, then more so can we do it for God, but we must have a vision and hold on to it regardless of what we go through.

The final quality is that of a positive self-image. You must know who you are as a woman of God. You will know if you keep yourself in the Word and prayer. Do not let your husband do all of the praying.

You pray! Talk to God about you until your esteem comes up. Women, keep yourselves looking nice. Your dress has a lot to do with how you feel on the inside. So, look good, talk good, and expect good things!

CHAPTER 6
Forming Relationships

It is known that much of one's success in life flows out of positive relationships. So, it is with a pastor's wife. It is important to establish relationships with people on our own level. We all need other people's help from time to time. The Lord never intended for any of us to be an island. I have found out as a pastor's wife that it is extremely beneficial to have quality friendships on our level.

A mistake many pastors' wives make is going to congregate and share their problems. First of all, we must remember that God has allowed us to be in a position of influence on the congregation and especially the women. Now, ladies, we know how women love to talk. Secondly, sharing personal problems with someone not on your level can cause them not to look up to your leadership, distrust you, and not respect your authority. Please remember whether you preach the Word or not, you are in a position of influence merely because you are a pastor's wife.

Therefore, we must develop relationships with other pastors' wives. Break out of your shells and get to know other women experiencing the same trials and tests you are. If you do not continue to grow, how do you expect the ladies in your church to grow? Now I am not advocating that you cannot share certain things with some of the mature ladies in your congregation. Still, I am saying you must be careful. Keep in mind that the Lord has given you graces so that you may be strongly established as a pastor's wife. Let us face it, we have many opportunities to establish relationships: at revivals, conferences, when visiting other churches and when other churches visit you, and at women's conferences. Take advantage of these opportunities and know that other pastors' wives are looking for the same things you are looking for. The Lord already has women in a position to help refresh your heart in the things of God. Your part is to reach out and start the relationship.

Many pastors' wives do not reach out to establish relationships

with other women in ministry because of an identity crisis. Let us talk about this. If you have not or do not work on developing personal confidence in your role, you will more than likely not want to hang out with women who have. Amos 3:3 declares, "Can two walks together, except they are agreed."

Ladies, let us remember that no one starts out in maturity. The women you see flowing strong beside their husbands are the ones who have grown alongside their husbands. Often lies the problem we have not grown with our husbands.

You probably will not be praying and studying as much as your husband, but you should still have a strong, devotional life. It is also wise for you to get with him and allow him to pour into you what God has poured into him. Remember, the man is to give us seed, then we are to incubate and give life to it. Your walk with God and the relationship of being a joint heir with your husband should help produce a strong identity in you as a pastor's wife. In my case, my husband acknowledges me as called alongside him in the ministry. We pastor together. He is not intimidated by me being right beside him, and I do not try to usurp authority where it has not been given.

Many pastors' wives are hurt and are intimidated by starting relationships with other women of God because they do not feel the support they need from their husbands. Show your husband that you are here to be his helpmeet and that you will do whatever you can to help the vision God has given to him come to pass. He will help you establish a strong identity in your role.

If you are an aggressive woman, then be cautious of your actions. Men do not like to be disrespected, nor do they like you assuming authority in areas that have not been given to you. Walk-in wisdom with your pastor-husband, and he will not mind helping affirm your identity and authority as a pastor's wife. Of course, he cannot do it all. There are some things we must do as well. However, get over the identity crisis and get some relationships started. We need one another's wisdom, faith, and encouragement. As we rally to strengthen one another, I believe that we will strengthen our husbands and help further the work of God in our areas.

As every Christian needs a Paul (Father), a Barnabas (friend), and a Timothy (son) in the things of God, so do we as pastors' wives need pastors' wives who are more mature than us. These friends are on our level and daughters in a pastor's wife position into whom we can pour. If we do not establish relationships now, then the generation of pastors' wives coming behind us will have to start from nothing, just like many of us have done in the role of a pastor's wife. The younger ones need our example. Paul admonished Titus to tell the "aged" (more matured) women to teach the younger. This principle applies to being an example to younger (less mature, just starting out) wives of pastors as it does to newly married women towards their husbands.

As a word of caution, relationship building should have a godly motive. It is not running down the church or forming gossip clubs. It should not be to run down your husband because he is not doing things the way you think they should be done. Our relationships and meetings should be for edification, comfort, and sharing the wisdom of God to help fulfill our roles.

CHAPTER 7
Dealing with Men and Women in the Church

Follow peace will all men, and holiness, without which no man shall see the Lord.

Hebrews 12:14

The work of the Lord is a people business. To be effective, you must get involved with people. You must get to know them. As a pastor's wife, you will, to some degree, have to deal with men and women depending upon how active you are in the ministry. Again, we need wisdom in dealing with both.

When it comes to dealing with men, simply treat them with respect. Do not let your position of influence as "the pastor's wife" cause you to be disrespectful toward men. I have known pastors' wives who have said, "I'm not taking anything off anyone, man or woman." These women often use their position to belittle and emasculate men because of some hurt they received from their father, uncle, or some past male relationship. It should not be that when you come around, the men quickly move away for fear of a "brassy" talking woman. Treat the brothers with respect. Leave the disciplining of men to your husband (unless you happen to be the senior Pastor). It is wise for you to have your husband or some mature churchmen be in on the discipline. Many men are already struggling with areas of their manhood, and they sure do not need you to put them down. In fact, you should allow the "motherly spirit" in you to be ushered from your bowels toward the brethren in your church. The motherly Spirit does not seek to castrate his manhood but build it up. You will be an effective pastor's wife if you sincerely seek to build people up.

The counseling of men should be left to their husbands. Never, never counsel a man by yourself. The bible commands us to "not let our good be evil spoken of." Countless pastors' wives have fallen into adultery because of unwise dealings with men. Do not become a statistic. Men will admire you when you are godly, but you must remember you have a God to please and a husband to satisfy. Keep yourself holy. Promotion from God will come to you and your husband when you live right.

Now let us talk about dealing with the sisters. You know as well as I do that dealing with the sisters is an entirely different ball game. In many churches, this is where the major problems lie. Regardless of how difficult some people may be, we must realize that they are God's sheep and will need to be mothered and mentored into God's will for their lives.

Ladies, please remember that you have a responsibility allotted to you by God to touch the women's lives in your church. If you stay before the Lord, he will give you a pearl of wisdom that will enable you to deal with whoever comes across the pathway of your life. Titus 2:3-5 reminds us of our responsibilities:

Likewise, the aged women are in behavior as becometh holiness, not false accusers, not given to much wine, teachers of good things. That they teach (train) the young women to be sober, to love their husbands, to love their children. To be discreet, chaste, keepers (workers) at home, good (kind), obedient to their own husbands, that the Word of God be not blasphemed.

The aged women refer to the spiritually old women by age or wisdom and possibly those out front in a position to influence or teach others. Since you are in the position, you just as well use it to glorify God. God has given every woman married to a pastor certain gifts, talents, or abilities. Use what you have, and God will increase it and give you more favor with women in your church.

Let us examine some more key points from the above passage of scripture. Paul admonished that the aged women train the younger women to love their husbands and children. You may say, "Some of the women in my church do some of the silliest things." Before judging and criticizing, you must get to know them and determine what measure they have been taught and trained. People simply will not know if they have not been taught. Do not assume anything and find out for yourself about women you have questions about.

You will be surprised at how an understanding and empathetic approach will cause a person to open up to you and long for your help. Another critical point that Paul (the writer of the book of Titus) brings out is that the aged are to teach the younger to be discreet. Being discreet has to do with being intelligent or wise in our dealings. The younger will learn to be wise if we do not take time with them and pour into them the wisdom God has given and continues to give us.

Ladies, please listen to me; being a pastor's wife and influencing other people for the glory of God will not be burdensome if we remember that God has caused us to have the position and that he is with us to help us as we look unto him. Our Father has great rewards on earth and in Heaven for women who are willing and obedient to God's will as pastors' wives.

My husband has taught me that knowledge aforehand helps relieve you of a lot of stress and mistakes. Knowledge about the diverse types of women who will come to your church will be of priceless value to you. Let me share my testimony with you. When the Lord called my husband and me to start pastoring, I first asked God about my part as a pastor's wife (although my husband says I have been called to Pastor alongside him). I wanted to glorify God in the position that he had given me. Whether I liked it, I realized that God has allowed me another positional opportunity to glorify him.

Actually, I have a dual role in the ministry. My first opportunity, as well as yours, was being a

Christian (someone Christ-like). My second opportunity is to be a wife, then a mother, and now a pastor's wife. Being a pastor's wife and then being Co-Pastor or Assistant Pastor to my husband. My husband says that he has no problem with me being his co- Pastor because of my submission to him as his wife. Of course, God and my husband have other requirements and standards that I have to meet as co-pastor with my husband.

Ladies know this, your husbands will take you further in the things of ministry if you provide yourselves submissive and helpful as a wife and open to learning and following the Lord's ways. Whatever your position is, glorify God in it, and he will bring promotion to your life.

When it came to dealing with the women in the church, I know that dealing with the women requires a different anointing of wisdom from what I have heard over the years. Ladies, you must pray for wisdom to deal with the diverse types of women who come into your church. I have personally chosen to look at the women in our church as daughters. The way you perceive someone has a lot to do with how you will treat them.

Let me talk to you about a few of the distinct types of women that will come into your church. First, the woman who wants the will of God in her life (married or single, she is sold out to God). You will not usually have any problems with this type of woman. Because of her zeal

She focuses on the Lord and "things above" to please God. Secondly, the woman who desires to please God is often sidetracked because of an impatient desire for male companionship. Thirdly, there is the woman who is married but hurting. Her marriage is in a wreck (usually, her husband is unsaved), but she keeps pressing her way to church. Fourthly, there is the woman who has never been fathered or mothered. She sometimes does not know how to dress without showing everything. She also does not know how to carry herself respectfully around men. She does not feel secure with herself. Fifthly, the woman is after your man's attention and any other man's attention she can get. Proverbs talk about the adulteress, the clamorous woman, the simple and the foolish woman. All of these and other types of women could fit in this category.

Please understand that the list I have given you is not exhaustive. There are many other categories of women who will come to your church as women who have been raped, abused, misused, and need help. Do not allow fear, intimidation, insecurities, or whatever else to stop you from reaching out to the women in your church.

You may feel like you cannot deal with women, but if God could cause a donkey to talk, he can empower you to touch women's lives in your church. As pastors ' wives, it is time that we do our part. Many pastors have fallen into adultery trying to do a job that he was not assigned to do. The bible says that the "older women are to teach and train the younger." Stop being at ease in Zion, press beyond anything trying to prohibit you, and bless your church with what God has given **you**!

ADDITIONAL READING AND REFERENCE MATERIAL

God's Purpose for a Marriage

Thus, the heavens and the earth were finished, and all the host of them.

2 And on the seventh day, God ended his work which he had made, and he rested on the seventh day from all his work which he had made.

3 And God blessed the seventh day and sanctified it: because that in it he had rested from all his work which God created and made.

4 These are the generations of the heavens and of the earth when they were created, in the day that the Lord God made the earth and the heavens,

5 And every plant of the field before it was in the earth, and every herb of the field before it grew: for the Lord God had not caused it to rain upon the earth, and there was not a man to till the ground.

6 But there went up a mist from the earth and watered the whole face of the ground.

7 And the Lord God formed man of the dust of the ground and breathed into his nostrils the breath of life; and man became a living soul.

8 And the Lord God planted a garden eastward in Eden; and there he put the man whom he had formed.

9 And out of the ground made the Lord God to grow every tree that is pleasant to the sight, and good for food, the tree of life also in the midst of the garden, and the tree of knowledge of good and evil.

10 And a river went out of Eden to water the

garden; and from thence it was parted and became into four heads.

11 The name of the first is Pison: that is it which compasseth the whole land of Havilah, where there is gold;

12 And the gold of that land is good: there is bdellium and the onyx stone.

13 And the name of the second river is Gihon: the same is it that compasseth the whole land of Ethiopia.

14 And the name of the third river is Hiddekel: that is it which goeth toward the east of Assyria. And the fourth river is Euphrates.

15 And the Lord God took the man and put him into the garden of Eden to dress it and to keep it.

16 And the Lord God commanded the man, saying, of every tree of the garden thou mayest freely

eat:

17 But of the tree of the knowledge of good and evil, thou shalt not eat of it: for in the day that thou eatest thereof thou shalt surely die.

18 And the Lord God said, It is not good that the man should be alone; I will make him an help meet for him.

19 And out of the ground the Lord God formed every beast of the field, and every fowl of the air; and brought them unto Adam to see what he would call them: and whatsoever Adam called every living creature, that was the name thereof.

20 And Adam gave names to all cattle, and to the fowl of the air, and to every beast of the field; but for Adam there was not found an help meet for him.

21 And the Lord God caused a deep sleep to fall upon Adam, and he slept: and he took one of his ribs,

and closed up the flesh instead thereof;

22 And the rib, which the Lord God had taken from man, made he a woman, and brought her unto the man.

23 And Adam said, this is now bone of my bones, and flesh of my flesh: she shall be called woman, because she was taken out of Man.

24 Therefore shall a man leave his father and his mother and shall cleave unto his wife: and they shall be one flesh.

25 And they were both naked, the man and his wife, and were not ashamed.

Explanation

The Hebrew term for the phrase "help meet for him" (*'ezer kenegdo*) literally means "a helper suited to, worthy of, or corresponding to him." The King James translators rendered this phrase "help meet"—the Word meet in sixteenth-century English meaning "fitting" or "proper."

According to The American Heritage Dictionary, "In the 17th century the two words' help' and 'meet' in this passage were mistaken for one Word, applying to Eve, and thus 'helpmeet' came to mean 'a wife.' Then in the 18th century, in a misguided attempt to make sense of the Word, the spelling' helpmate' was introduced." (Second college edition, Boston: Houghton Mifflin, 1982, p. 604.)

So, what exactly does it mean to be a suitable helper? The key is the Word suitable. A suitable wife is compatible with her husband in many respects—physically, mentally, emotionally, and spiritually. This doesn't mean the man and woman are the same in everything, only that they fit together in harmony. They complement each other.

Is Marriage for Everyone?

Does it mean that every woman must be a wife and a completer of a man? No. Not every woman wants to marry or is led to matrimony. However, the Genesis passage sets the standard for most people in most contexts. A wife is the helper suitable for her husband.

1 Corinthians 7:7–9 (ESV): 7 I wish that all were as I myself am. But each has his own gift from God, one of one kind and one of another.

8 To the unmarried and the widows I say that it is good for them to remain single, as I am. 9 But if they cannot exercise self-control, they should marry.

For it is better to marry than to burn with passion.

A good Wife

Sayings of King Lemuel

31 The sayings of King Lemuel—an inspired utterance his mother taught him.

2 Listen, my son! Listen, son of my womb!

Listen, my son, the answer to my prayers!

3 Do not spend your strength[a] on women,

your vigor on those who ruin kings.

4 It is not for kings, Lemuel—

it is not for kings to drink wine,

not for rulers to crave beer,

5 lest they drink and forget what has been decreed and deprive all the oppressed of their rights.

6 Let beer be for those who are perishing,

wine for those who are in anguish!
7 Let them drink and forget their poverty
   and remember their misery no more.
8 Speak up for those who cannot speak for themselves,
   for the rights of all who are destitute.
9 Speak up and judge fairly;
   defend the rights of the poor and needy.

Epilogue: The Wife of Noble Character

10 A wife of noble character who can find?
   She is worth far more than rubies.
11 Her husband has full confidence in her
   and lacks nothing of value.
12 She brings him good, not harm,
   all the days of her life.
13 She selects wool and flax

and works with eager hands.

14 She is like the merchant ships,

bringing her food from afar.

15 She gets up while it is still night;

she provides food for her family

and portions for her female servants.

16 She considers a field and buys it;

out of her earnings she plants a vineyard.

17 She sets about her work vigorously;

her arms are strong for her tasks.

18 She sees that her trading is profitable,

and her lamp does not go out at night.

19 In her hand she holds the distaff

and grasps the spindle with her fingers.

20 She opens her arms to the poor

and extends her hands to the needy.

21 When it snows, she has no fear for her

household. for all of them are clothed in scarlet.

22 She makes coverings for her bed;
   she is clothed in fine linen and purple.
23 Her husband is respected at the city gate,
   where he takes his seat among the elders of the
land.
24 She makes linen garments and sells them,
   and supplies the merchants with sashes.
25 She is clothed with strength and dignity;
   she can laugh at the days to come.
26 She speaks with wisdom,
   and faithful instruction is on her tongue.
27 She watches over the affairs of her household
   and does not eat the bread of idleness.
28 Her children arise and call her blessed;
   her husband also, and he praises her:
29 "Many women do noble things,

but you surpass them all."

30 Charm is deceptive, and beauty is fleeting;

but a woman who fears the Lord is to be praised.

31 Honor her for all that her hands have done,

and let her works bring her praise at the city gate.

Qualities of Godly Leadership

Servant's Heart

Matthew 23:11 (ESV): 11 The greatest among you shall be your servant.

Teachable

Proverbs 19:20 (ESV): 20 Listen to advice and

accept instruction, that you may gain wisdom in the future.

Filled with the Holy Spirit

Acts 6:3 (ESV): 3 Therefore, brothers, pick out from among you seven men of good repute, full of the Spirit and of wisdom, whom we will appoint to this duty.

Enthusiastic about his role

Ephesians 6:7 (ESV): 7 rendering service with a good will as to the Lord and not to man,

A model of humility and forgiveness

1 Peter 5:6 (ESV): 6 Humble yourselves, therefore, under the mighty hand of God so that at the proper time he may exalt you,

Ephesians 4:32 (ESV): 32 Be kind to one another, tenderhearted, forgiving one another, as God in Christ forgave you.

Loving to those he leads

Matthew 5:46 (ESV): 46 For if you love those who love you, what reward do you have? Do not even the tax collectors do the same?

John 13:34-35 (ESV): 34 A new commandment I give to you, that you love one another: just as I have loved you, you also are to love one another. 35 By this all people will know that you are my disciples if you have love for one another."

Ready to admit his failures and areas where he needs growth

Philippians 3:12 (ESV): 12 Not that I have already obtained this or am already perfect, but I press on to make it my own, because Christ Jesus has made me his own.

Notes

____

Touching the Hearts of Pastors' Wives

Notes

Notes

Notes

About The Author Dr. Judy Ellison

Since the fall of Adam and Eve, marriage has been in a ceaseless battle for its potential, glory and even its existence. We see from the study of scripture that not only was Satan out to separate God and man, but also man and women. Obviously, Satan watched God and Adam walk powerfully together for some time and figured that if he was going to have a shot at ruling the earth, then he had to cause a disruption between the two.

Well, not only did he disrupt the primary source of divine power from flowing through the earth (the relationship between God and man, but the secondary as well (the unity of man and woman).

Therefore, we can see that not only did Satan closely observe God and man's relationship and see power, but he also closely observed the power of relationship between a man and woman. You see, God did not give Adam rulership over the earth until Eve came on the scene. You are probably saying, "Well, what did Adam rule until that time?" We will tell you – the Garden of Eden. God originally intended that earth be patterned after Heaven. In Heaven you have corporate rule under the leadership of God the Father. Earth, likewise, was to be ruled corporately under the leadership of the man.

When Satan attacked marriage in the Garden of Eden, a major part of his intent was to destroy the image of corporate rule in the earth. He did not want to see multitudes of husbands and wives becoming replicas of unity in the earth realm. He did not want to see the generation of children beholding the image of a husband and wife ruling together. Don't be mistaken – image is "Everything". You will become what you constantly gaze upon. No wonder God told Israel to tear down all the graven images out of the lands of the heathens they conquered. Many divorces are the by-products of bad marriages that one or both spouses looked upon for years before they were married. Subconsciously then, the image of a bad marriage was stored in either or both of the spouse's minds and under the right circumstances (he or she) will begin acting out what was previously stored.

Many of the divorces of our day are the results of the "Bad Marriage" image being relived. We must destroy that image and begin displaying the image of a man and woman who are rightly related. Here we have it – a man and a woman, rightly related, reveals the image of God in the earth.

And God said, "Let us make man (male and

female corporately) in our image, after our likeness (of rulership and dominion): and let them have dominion over the fish of the sea, and over the foul of the air, and over the cattle, and over all the earth, and over every creeping thing that creepeth upon the earth." Genesis 1:26

9 798886 807424